home furnishing
workbook

home furnishing *workbook*

Katrin Cargill

photography by **James Merrell**

RYLAND

PETERS

& SMALL

This edition first published in the
USA in 2001

by Ryland Peters & Small, Inc
519 Broadway, 5th Floor
New York, NY 10012
www.rylandpeters.com

10 9 8 7 6 5 4 3 2 1

Printed and bound in China

ISBN 1-84172-148-4

Senior designers
Paul Tilby and Larraine Shamwana

Designers
Sally Powell and Ingunn Jensen

Senior editors
Annabel Morgan and Sian Parkhouse

Editors
**Maddalena Bastianelli, Toria Leitch,
Sophie Pearse and Miriam Hyslop**

Design assistants
Luis Peral-Aranda and Mark Latter

Production
Patricia Harrington

Illustrators
**Michael Hill, Jacqueline Pestell and
Lizzie Sanders**

The material contained in this book was
originally published in four different titles:
Lampshades and *Pillows* (both published in
1996) and *Bed Linens* and *Simple Curtains*
(both published in 1998).

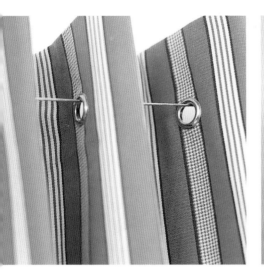

contents

Luckily, the recent trend toward less cluttered, busy interiors means we no longer need to spend a fortune buying yards of fabric to festoon our homes. Nowadays, clean lines, appealing textures, and strong colors make a much more sophisticated statement than acres of stiff brocade, rows of flouncy frills, or overelaborate trimmings. Grandeur and formality have made way for a new, inviting mood of simplicity and freshness.

However, if this new look of understated elegance is to be effective, it does demand a certain amount of attention to detail, quality, and finish. You may need less fabric to make these new home furnishings, but because the items are more simple and unadorned, the fabric should be the very best you can afford, in exactly the right color and texture for your room. And just a few finishing touches—the special trimming on a lampshade, perhaps, or velvet piping on a cushion—will turn a humble homemade item into a piece of furnishing *haute couture*.

Another important factor is choosing exactly the right curtain, bedspread, lampshade, or cushion for your room. Try to be sensitive to the dimensions and proportions of your home. In a tiny space, allow understated but elegant drapes or a luxurious bedspread to be the single central focus. In a larger room, you can afford to add

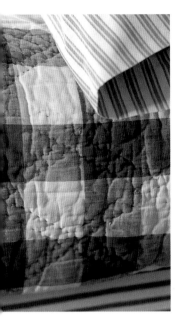

a few more elements—combine a couple of plump, inviting pillows with well-chosen lampshades and a pair of softly gathered curtains to enliven your interior.

In this book, I have put together a collection of varied ideas to inspire you to create elegant and stylish rooms. There are hundreds of imaginative suggestions for you to make at home, whatever your level of skill, and 32 fully illustrated projects that clearly explain how to achieve entirely professional results. These projects can easily be adapted to suit your own color scheme or scaled up or down to suit the proportions of your home.

The key message in all the projects and ideas is to keep them simple and pay attention to detail and quality—it is far better to make a plain cushion in a wonderfully luxurious fabric than to complicate it by adding overambitious trimmings or an excess of details. By the same token, the effect on a room of a pair of unlined curtains in a heavy, good-quality fabric, hung from a sturdy wooden or metal pole, is far superior to heavily lined and interlined drapes with ornate valances and swags and tails, which will only catch the dust and dirt and are horribly difficult to clean.

Happy sewing and decorating!
Katrin Cargill

bed linen

above left Checks and stripes in combination are unified by the use of a blue and white color scheme throughout.
left Delicate white thread embroidery enlivens the edges of a crisp cotton sheet and matching pillowcase.
below left Using ties as a fastening is a simple solution to closing covers and cases, as well as an attractive decorative addition. Either make them in a contrasting fabric or use the same material for a more subtle form of embellishment.

top right The simple geometric designs of the decorative stitching on these pillowcases perfectly complements the colors and shapes of the patchwork bedspread.
above right A hot pink flanged border adds a bold and colorful note to an otherwise plain pair of white pillowcases.
below right The regimented stripes and precisely squared ends of this plump bolster are the perfect match for the bedspread beneath, giving the bed an air of tailored elegance.

above Quilted fabric with an unusual textural quality adds interest to a pillow and creates a cozy, comfortable feel.
left Linen pillowcases and sheets are the ultimate luxury. This linen pillowcase is held closed by floppy linen bows, a soft, informal look perfect for a bedroom.

pillows and sheets A bedroom is

a place for sleep, but it is also a room where you can be a little self-indulgent with your forms of decoration. Don't just stick to the usual plain bed dressings, but instead use checks or stripes to add a simple yet eye-catching area of interest. If this seems too adventurous, introduce more subtle decorative touches, such as an embroidered or contrasting border running around the edges of sheets, or ties and buttoning on pillows.

above left Lacy delicate cutwork on starched white cotton is a bed linen classic. Here, a pretty daisy pattern adorns the border of a large square pillowcase.
above right An impromptu bolster case is constructed from a piece of white cotton loosely tied with a peach satin ribbon.
left A dainty drawn threadwork border embellishes these matching pillowcases. The crisp cool cotton of the bed linen is teamed with a vivid red bedspread for a cozy countrified effect.

piqué pillows
with bows

These invitingly plump brown gingham pillowcases are extremely easy
to make, especially if you use extra-wide sheeting fabric, as you will
need only a single piece of fabric that is twice the width of the pillow.
The piqué panels, held in place with matching gingham bows, lend the
pillowcases a demure air of modesty and old-fashioned charm.

materials & equipment

cotton gingham fabric

cotton piqué fabric

1 To calculate fabric quantities, measure the width and length of your pillow (see Techniques, page 176). The fabric must be twice the width of the pillow plus an additional 10½ in. for the flap and the seam allowances, and the same length as the pillow plus 1¼ in. seam allowance. Cut out the fabric (see Techniques, page 177).

2 Place the fabric on a flat surface, right side up. Along the short edges of the fabric, press a double ⅜ in. hem to the wrong side. Pin, baste, and machine stitch both the hems in place. Measure 8 in. in from one hemmed end and press a fold to the wrong side of the fabric. This fold will form the pocket flap that holds the pillow snugly in the case.

3 Fold the fabric in half across the width with right sides together. The hemmed short end must be on top, and the end with the pressed flap underneath. Line up the hemmed edge of the fabric with the pressed fold of the flap. Now bring the flap up and over so it covers the hemmed edge and lies on top of the folded pillowcase.

4 Pin, baste, and machine stitch all the way along the long sides of the pillowcase, stitching ⅝ in. from the raw edges. Reinforce and strengthen the sides of the pocket flap by stitching a second seam on top of the first one.

5 Trim any excess fabric from each corner and, using zigzag stitch, machine stitch around the raw edges of the fabric to prevent them from fraying. Turn the pillowcase right side out.

6 Each pillowcase has eight ties. Cut eight strips of gingham, each measuring 1 x 13 in., and make the ties (see Techniques, page 183). Cut the gingham strips on the bias (see Techniques, page 183)— the ties will look decorative and have more "give."

red-trimmed
linen

Cool linen sheets and pillowcases are irresistibly inviting after a long
day. Here, square pillows have been encased in linen pillowcases
trimmed with boldly colored faggoting for a cozy, country effect.
Teamed with a matching sheet and a simple gingham bedspread,
they bring a charming air of simplicity to a bedroom.

materials & equipment

white cotton or linen fabric

¾-in-wide trim

7 On the front of the pillowcase, mark a point 5 in. on each side of each corner and 2 in. in from the edges. Fold the ties in half and pin, then hand stitch them securely in place.

8 Cut out a piece of cotton piqué exactly the same size as your finished pillowcase. Press a ½ in. fold to the wrong side around all four edges. Now turn in a second 1¼ in. fold along all four sides. Miter the corners (see Techniques, page 183). Pin, baste, and machine stitch the hems in place, 1 in. from the outside edge.

9 Place the pillowcase on a flat surface and position the piqué panel on top, making sure it is exactly centered. Using a fabric pen, lightly mark two lines on the piqué above each tie, each ¼ in. long and ½ in. apart. In total, there should be 16 lines above 8 ties.

10 Remove the panel from the pillowcase and carefully cut slits along each marked line. Finish and strengthen each slit with buttonhole stitch (see Techniques, page 182). Thread the ends of the ties through the buttonholes of the piqué panel, and tie in a bow.

7 Check that the ribbons run straight and are exactly parallel to each other. Machine stitch them in place along both edges, stitching in the same direction along each side to prevent the ribbon from puckering.

8 Repeat steps 6 and 7 with another four strips of ribbon, this time positioning the ribbons so their upper long edge aligns with the horizontal marked lines on the bedspread.

9 Turn in and press a ¼ in. hem to the right side all around the edges of the bedspread.

10 There should be four strips of ribbon left to border the bedspread. At each end of the first strip, fold the ribbon diagonally to the wrong side at a 45° angle. Press in place. Repeat this procedure with the three remaining lengths of ribbon.

11 Place the first strip right side up along one edge of the bedspread over the hemmed edges of the fabric, aligning the folded edge of the bedspread with the outside edge of the ribbon. Pin and baste in place. Repeat along the next edge of the bedspread. At the corners, the pressed diagonal edges should meet up exactly to form a miter.

12 When the ribbon is basted in place around the four sides of the bedspread, machine stitch down both sides of the ribbon. Make sure each seam is stitched in the same direction so the ribbon does not pucker.

13 Slipstitch the mitered corners of the ribbon closed. Press the bedspread and place it on the bed.

1 Cut out the fabric and join widths if necessary, using a flat fell seam (see Techniques, page 183). Make sure you have a full-width panel set in the center of the bedspread with equal part-widths on each side.

2 Cut the blue-striped ribbon into 12 equal lengths of exactly 85 in. each.

3 Lay the bedspread on a flat surface, right side up. Mark a line running the whole length of the bedspread,17 in. from the left-hand side of the fabric.

4 Mark three more vertical lines across the fabric at 17 in. intervals. The last line should be 17 in. from the right-hand side of the bedspread.

5 Still working on the right side of the bedspread, mark a horizontal line 17 in. down from the top edge of the bedspread. Mark another three lines at 17 in. intervals down the bedspread. Use a drawing square to check that the horizontal lines are at an exact 90° angle to the vertical stripes.

6 Take the first length of ribbon and place it on top of the bedspread, the left-hand edge of the ribbon aligned with the first vertical line running down the bedspread. Pin and baste in place down the length of the bedspread. Repeat across the bedspread until there are 4 lengths of ribbon basted vertically in place.

feather-stitched patchwork quilt

This cozy patchwork quilt, made from scraps and remnants of antique blue and white printed cotton, is not handstitched in the traditional way. Instead, the quilt is machine-sewn to save time and effort. Feather stitching in a complementary color scrambles over and around the seams, providing a decorative finishing touch.

materials & equipment

a wide variety of scraps and remnants of fabric for the patchwork

batting

backing fabric for the quilt

embroidery needle

silk embroidery thread

dust ruffles serve a practical purpose, concealing

unattractive bed bases, stumpy bed legs, and underbed storage areas.
Overelaborate specimens made in flouncy, fussy designs have earned dust
ruffles a bad reputation. However, it is undeserved, for a tailored example
with inverted pleats can be extremely elegant, while a delicate lace-trimmed
one made from antique cotton sheets will add distinction to any bedroom.

left and above Fine organza
with a deep double hem
billows out beneath a simple
wooden-framed bed.
Despite its fragile, flimsy
appearance, organza is
extremely strong, making it
a luxurious yet practical
choice for home furnishings.
below In a guest bedroom,
a blue and white theme
combines checks, stripes,
and flowers, and
demonstrates how different
patterns can be harmoniously
linked by color alone.
This stylish effect has been
achieved on a tight budget—
the dust ruffles are fashioned
from humble dish towels.

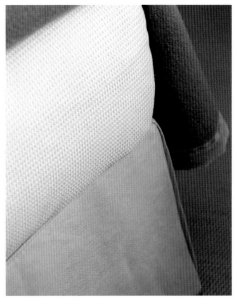

above The graphic lines and chunky red and white blocks of this check dust ruffle are softened by the unexpected addition of a dainty white lace trim at the top.
below left and right A colorful red and white cotton check is sewn into precise box pleats in this cheerful dust ruffle, which makes the bed the focal point in this small bedroom.

bottom left A delicate white scalloped sheet used as a dust ruffle hangs just above floor level, peeping out from under an exquisitely detailed quilted bedspread.
above right A simple yet sophisticated linen dust ruffle with an inverted pleat at the corners adds a unfussy note of comfort to a cool contemporary interior.

tailored pictorial print

Toile de Jouy, a cotton fabric printed with idyllic pastoral scenes
in muted tones, is ideally suited to a relaxed and soothing bedroom
environment. If it is made into frilly bed dressings, the effect can be a
little too "cute." However, *toile de Jouy* is ideally suited to the simple
uncluttered lines of this chic, precisely pleated dust ruffle.

materials & equipment

toile de Jouy *fabric*

lining fabric

cording

bias binding (the same color as the piping cord)

appliquéd zigzags

This bold dust ruffle, with its zigzag edges, strikes a note of warmth and vitality in an otherwise cool and uncluttered bedroom. The hot pink color and solid shapes of the skirt are a perfect foil for the graceful fluid outline of an antique brass bedstead. A down-home check fabric, which harmonizes perfectly with the pink of the skirt, has been used for the duvet and cut into squares that are applied to the skirt on point to make diamonds.

materials & equipment

plain cotton fabric

checked cotton or gingham

lining fabric

canopies add drama and romance to a bedroom. Even an ordinary divan can be transformed by the addition of flowing drapes. A corona creates a formal, elegant effect, while a simple mosquito net suspended above the bed will add a hint of colonial style. What could be more soothing than drifting off to sleep cocooned in layers of gently flowing fabric?

left and above A fine organza canopy softens the hard lines of a metal bed. The fabric has been sewn to a hoop that is suspended from the ceiling. Narrow gold velvet ribbon is stitched to the outside edges of the canopy, adding a touch of luxury to a cool white scheme. The crisp white cotton bed linen is edged in matching gold ribbon, unifying the scheme.
right A magnificent Shaker cherrywood fourposter is adorned with a panel of bold checks and subtle stripes, loosely knotted to a horizontal support. The practical ties mean that the panel can be easily removed for seasonal changes or laundering.

left and above A modern metal fourposter with clean minimalist lines is softened with delicate drapery made from hemmed organza and an intricate lace bedspread, which create an ethereal feel without concealing the elegant lines of the bed.

41

scalloped corona

A corona brings a regal and elegant air to any bed, and has the
ability to transform the most ordinary of bedrooms into a luxurious
retreat. The elegant carved-wood corona shown in the picture below
is a traditional Swedish design. Similar ready-made coronas can
be difficult to find, so here I show how to create the effect using
a corona board made from plywood and concealed by a scalloped
valance, which adds a majestic finishing touch.

materials & equipment

¾ in. thick plywood for the corona board

angle brackets

flexible curtain track

curtain hooks

woven checked cotton fabric

1 in. wide gathering tape

¾ in. wide velcro

tie-on bed curtains

Four-posters are often associated with grand, formal beddressings, but here the austere lines of a very contemporary metal-framed four-poster are softened by eight cotton bed curtains loosely tied to the top of the bed frame. As both sides of the hangings are visible, a woven check fabric has been used to dispense with the need for lining.

materials & equipment

thick Madras cotton check

bias binding in a contrasting color

cushions

left A rectangular cushion in a green and white striped cotton has an exaggerated, plumply padded border in a plain brushed cotton.
below A trio of shapes: a heart outlined with a heavy chenille fringe; a tailored boxed triangle emphasised by thin dark piping; and a narrow bolster in a woven linen check.

shapes
Mention the word "cushion" and what probably springs to mind is a typical box shape. Although there are some differently shaped cushions available ready-made, if you are prepared to hunt for more unusual forms of pad, or better still make your own shaped forms by simply stuffing a pad you have sewn yourself, then you can create original cushions in any number of shapes.

A mattress effect is created by deep buttoning right through to the back of these cushions. Great for benches and stools.

above Star struck: this three-dimensional shape can provide the only pattern on a plain sofa or chair.

left from top Bobble fringe in a deeper contrasting color livens up a solid fabric; box cubes made from brushed cotton suit a modern interior; green plaid squares echo the square shape of this cushion, which has Turkish corners caught together with thin, darker green piping; a football shaped pillow made from four panels, with contrasting piping, looks ready to fly through the air; square of squares: a woven linen check and viscose fabric with a tightly gathered little ruffled edge.

below A rectangle of horizontal stripes in cotton outlined with a bottle-green wool bobble fringe.

the star

This shape brings an unusual accent to a decorative scheme.
It may not be one to curl up on for cozy reading, but a strongly
contrastingly colored star or two can provide a wonderful focus in a
room. It may be tricky to find a template for this shape, but it is easy to
make your own using a satisfyingly simple mathematical process.
This star is made from a cotton check with an embroidered floral motif
and is corded in a narrow contrasting color for extra emphasis.

materials & equipment

48 in. checked cotton, 44 in. wide

contrasting fabric to make 2 ¾ yd. cording

2 ¾ yd. extra thin piping cord, ⅛ in. wide

kapok stuffing (or equivalent)

a sheet of paper 23 x 23 in.

protractor

drawing compass

bobbles in the round

Circular pads are readily available, though they tend to be of the pancake variety. This pill-shaped size can lend itself to both traditional or modern situations. Here a creamy spotted voile looks almost ethereal with the addition of two rows of cotton bobble fringe. Making it can be tricky, so follow the steps carefully.

materials & equipment

1 ¾ yd. spotted voile fabric, 60 in. wide

2 ¾ yd. piping cord

2 ¾ yd. bobble fringe

15 in. round pillow form, 14 in. deep

contrasting-colored basting thread

above left A white wool bobble fringe trims a strong animal print of heavy beige and red woven cotton.

above center An exquisitely delicate cut velvet and chenille tassel in rich shades of purple and gold dangles on the corner of a woven organdy ribbon cushion.

above right The harlequin pattern of this fabric emphasizes the long bolster shape of the cushion. The edges are trimmed with a cotton tasseled fringe.

right This very impressive cushion is made from burgundy wool. The regal-looking crest is stitched directly onto the front and is set off beautifully by the rich gold metallic cording with looped corners.

above Gaufraged golden thistles on a wine-colored velvet, edged in two-tone rope and tassels.

left A patchwork of rich and sumptuous silks, separated by a golden metallic ribbon, edged in a multicolored tasseled fringe.

below left A cotton and gaufraged velvet stripe looks chic with chenille fringe.

below center Rich woven damask needs the adornment of only a thin rope border.

below right Jewel-colored wool and mohair to keep you warm.

use of fabrics

There is a bewildering choice of fabrics available. However, if you think beyond the three basic elements of any fabric—color, pattern, and texture—you will see that there are all sorts of ways you can play with these elements for decorative effect. By piecing together clever contrasts and combinations of fabrics, you can achieve spectacular results.

top A lush harlequin velvet cushion with novel tassels sits atop a knife-edged golden cotton damask cushion.
above Antique needlepoint cushions are very popular, and harder and harder to find. This lovely example is trimmed with golden ribbon and a tasseled fringe.
left Variations on a color theme: burgundy and grass green in different textures— above, inexpensive display felt, and below, rough burlap.

stripes into
squares

A pillow to add a touch of imperial style to a day bed or sofa.
Link the material and tassel to other color themes in the room, or
perhaps let it stand alone to make a bold statement in what might
otherwise be a somewhat dull corner. Here, construction and design
rely on four triangles mitered together into a square.

materials & equipment

1 ½ yd. striped cotton, 45 in. wide

Four 7-in. lengths of thick piping cord

decorative tassel

18 in. pillow form

ruler

right A finely woven pure white linen cushion has a surface-applied fringe made of natural hemplike string. *below* Three rows of deep natural cotton fringe cover the surface of cream cotton to make a funky cushion.

trimmings and fastenings

Unadorned, a cushion tends to blend into the seating or surface it is placed upon. To make a feature of the cushion itself calls for some clever ideas to dress up the basic shape. Choose from the wealth of decorative trimmings and fastenings available to embellish cushions in dozens of ways.

above Three examples of back fastening ties: finished with knots; secured by square tabs of the fabric; doubled cotton with zigzag edges.
far left A striped silk cushion has a doubled ruffled edge, finished with a pleated satin ribbon.
left For a neat finish on this plaid cushion, the fan edging has been box-pleated at each of the corners.

top left A crewelwork cushion is trimmed in dark green linen fringe.
left below The diamond shape and the circular patchwork detail are outlined by rows of tiny bobble fringe in dark purple.

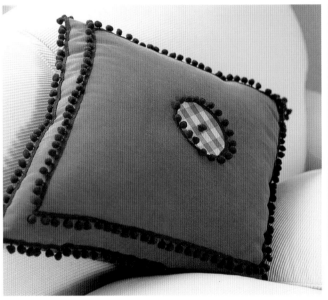

above Buttons and tufts: silk looped button; deep tufted linen; a wonderful antique handsewn button; a tuft made from cutting a square piece of fabric with pinking shears.
left Two rectangles: one has a natural ruched fringe to contrast with the subtle plaid, the other is finished in a two-tone fan edging with four tufted linen buttons sewn down each side.

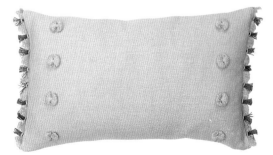

rope-edged knotted cushion

A cool Indian Madras pillow is paired with a bright red rope border, sewn directly onto the edge of the cover. The extended corners are long enough to be knotted, to create a fresh and different look. A pile of pillows in inexpensive contrasting Madras fabrics can look gloriously exuberant.

materials & equipment

2 ¼ yd. cotton fabric, 45 in. wide

5 ½ yd. rope edging

18 in. square pillow form

pattern paper, 40 in. square

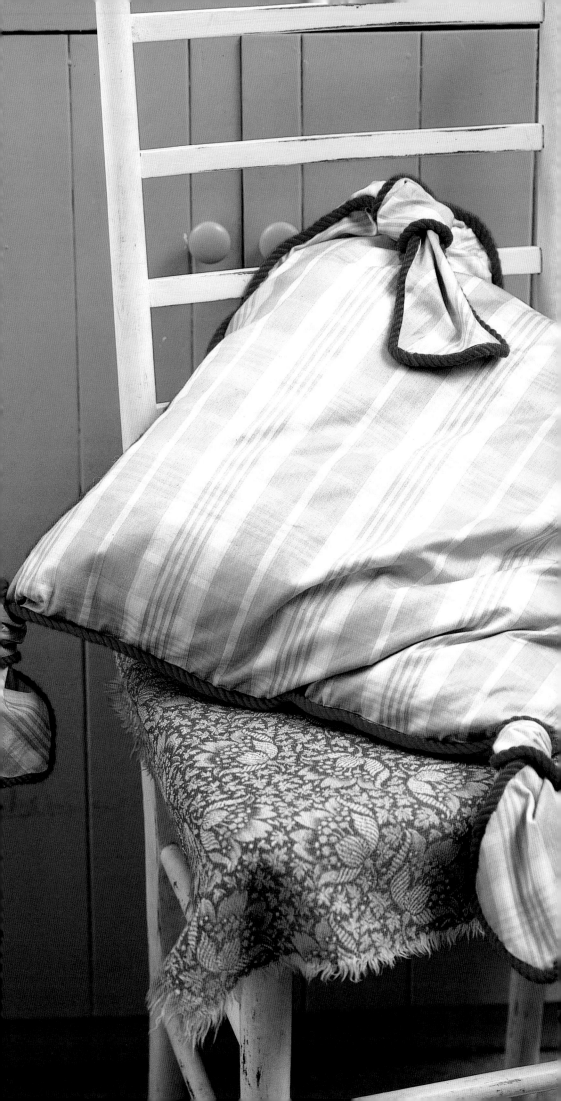

fastened with tassels

In this formal design, pure white linen encases a silk inner lining to create a sleek and sophisticated cushion. These luxurious fabrics are appropriately dressed up with a pair of silk tassels that provide an elegant means of fastening and the open end of the linen casing is delicately edged with drawn thread work.

materials & equipment

20 in. cream even-weave linen, 45 in. wide

1 yd. striped silk, 45 in. wide

two silk tassels

16 in. square pillow form

82

loose
linen cover

Two squares of cool striped beige linen with pairs of ties on each
side hold an inner pillow covered in contrasting striped fabric.
An easy-to-make cushion that will create a big impact, this idea is
excellent for giving a quick facelift to older pillows that
are beginning to look a little tired.

materials & equipment

24 in. beige-stripe linen fabric, 45 in. wide

20 in. red-stripe cotton fabric, 45 in. wide

5 yd. cotton tape in brown, 1 in. wide

5 yd. cotton tape in cream, ⅝ in. wide

18 in. square pillow pad

far left Hand-stitched parallel rows of white knitting yarn create a bold pattern on black wool.
left Black on white felt—painstakingly arranged circles have been cut out to provide the pattern on this white inner pillow.

surface decoration

For those who want to be challenged beyond running up cushion covers on a sewing machine—or indeed for those who enjoy the slower pace of stitching by hand—there are numerous ways of applying surface decoration to your own or ready-made pillows. Cross stitch, embroidery, quilting, and appliqué can all be used to add decorative and personal touches.

right A brown boiled-wool cushion has been intricately embroidered with folk-art multicolored flowers and finished with an edging of thick red rope.
below right Cream linen has been bordered in cross-stitched black embroidery thread; the back of the pillow is black-and-white gingham check.
below A corner detail of a wool and velvet ribbon patchwork cushion.

above A satin stitch heart embroidered in heavy yarn on fine cream flannel.
left from top Leftover fabrics and a carefully cut initial appliquéd together; strong yellow ovals of yarn in satin stitch outlined in black; delicate flowers are intricately stitched onto cream linen; hand-painted silk makes an elegant pillow; embroidered leopard-skin needlepoint looks almost like the real thing!
below This brown knitted cushion has been tie-dyed and felted to give a unique finish, while the top cushion is a patchwork of velvet ribbon, knitted wool squares, and woven linen.

autumnal appliqué

Like many other forms of needlecraft, appliqué has survived for
generations and lends itself well to all manner of designs, both pictorial
and abstract. All you need to do is decide on a motif or series
of motifs, make a template, and cut them out from scraps
of fabric; then appliqué them to a background.

materials & equipment

20 in. heavy cotton fabric, 45 in. wide

¼ yd. contrasting fabric for the motif, 45 in. wide

18 in. square pillow form

¼ yd. iron-on fusible web, 45 in. wide

lampshades

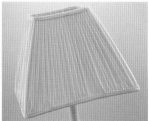

shapes

Lampshades come in all manner of shapes, and the outline of the basic frame is what gives the shade its intrinsic character. There are plenty of shapes to choose from, including drums and cylinders; cones of all sorts, from the more open Empire and coolie to the tall narrow chimney; bowed shades with a concave profile; or more solid-looking straight-sided shades, which may be hexagonal or boxlike, in the form of a gently tapering square or rectangle.

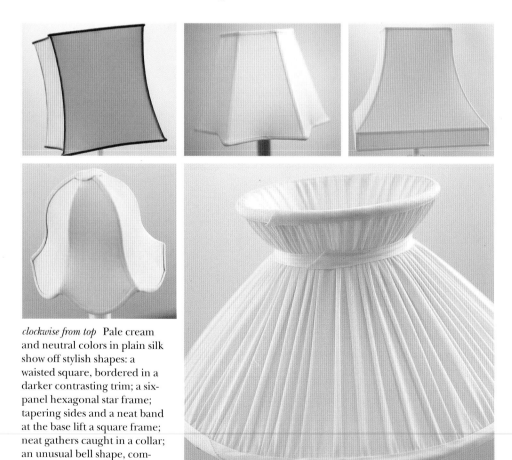

clockwise from top Pale cream and neutral colors in plain silk show off stylish shapes: a waisted square, bordered in a darker contrasting trim; a six-panel hexagonal star frame; tapering sides and a neat band at the base lift a square frame; neat gathers caught in a collar; an unusual bell shape, completely covered at the top.

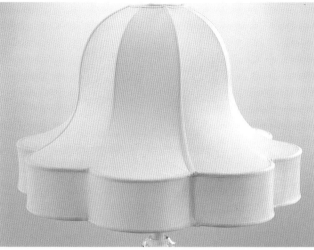

clockwise from top A large and impressive covered bell shade with a deeply banded base—a sturdy frame and a very pretty shape for a floor lamp; the standard coolie shape, like this gathered shade, works in any size, for floors or for tables; a wide bowed oval with a narrow waist and a ruffled edge (detail shown opposite); a collared Empire shade, finished with a plain band at the top and bottom and around the collar; pleated cotton flares out from a narrow circular opening at the top to a wider square base; a basic straight-sided Empire shade shows off tightly gathered silk to its best effect.

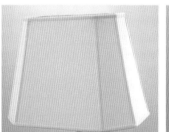

clockwise from top This elegant wavy-edge frame is covered in tightly pleated silk; an octagonal oblong shape with a Regency feel; a wide hexagonal shade allows plenty of light to shine out—ideal for a floor lamp; a wide gathered silk coolie shade; neat wide box pleats fan out over an elongated oval shade.

pleated coolie

A buttery yellow silk taffeta is tightly pleated all around the top of this small coolie, and the pleats fan out evenly around the gently flaring sides for a crisp clean effect. The lamp is then given a punchy finish with scarlet trimming around the top and bottom rings in the same rich fabric as the main body of the shade, for a strong contrast. The inner silk lining protects the outer cover and gives the whole design a highly professional finish.

materials & equipment

coolie frame with six struts and base gimbal fixture 4 in. diameter top; 10 in. diameter bottom; 5 in. height

20 in. silk lining, 45 in. wide

10 in. butter-yellow silk taffeta, 60 in. wide

3 x 37 in. strip of red silk taffeta

½ in. wide binding tape

above A small coolie-shaped top is edged in a deep band, covered by neat knife pleats of cream silk and lengthened by a silk fringe.

right from top Cotton ticking stripes meet perfectly across the angles of this paneled shade to form a chevron design; a lightweight cotton fabric has been dipped in fabric stiffener and then draped diagonally over an Empire shade for a sumptuous ruched effect; regal red crushed velvet is stiffened with lamination and trimmed with leather; the finest ecru silk is tightly gathered around a coolie shade and finished with a pinked skirt; moiré silk in contrasting colors complements the shaped panels of this stylish shade.

use of fabrics and trimmings

Second only to the shape of the lampshade, the type of fabric and trimming you choose to cover the frame will dictate the overall look of the shade. For instance, the same basic cone would look very different covered in a laminated striped cloth than if you decided on a loose, skirtlike cover in a floral print. Both heavy-and lightweight fabrics alike can be used to decorate lampshades.

left A crisp red-and-white cotton gingham is shown to best effect on a simple Empire shape. The geometric check accentuates the perfect knife pleats, which are finished with binding of the same checked fabric, used on the diagonal.
below from left Double pinked ruffles in a complementary fabric with a smaller motif edge this tighly gathered printed cotton shade; delicate cream lace is generously gathered and held in place over a plain cream shade by a pretty satin ribbon tied in a bow; this unusual shade is created using a thin printed cotton stiffened with lamination and then scored into shaped sections—bias binding finishes the raw edges and a ribbon threaded through the scored sections pulls the shade into tight gathers to form a petal pattern along the top edge.

above A coolie-shaped frame is covered in a tightly gathered printed cotton, and trimmed along the bottom edge with strongly contrasting wide cotton fringe.
right Checked voile is used as a loose cover over a collared Empire silk shade. The delicate fabric stands out stiffly from the smocked top, and the top and bottom edges are finished in red velvet piping.

skirted pictorial print

Patterned fabrics work as well as plains, particularly on loose fabric lampshades. Here, a pretty red and white *toile de Jouy* is sewn into a full, pleated skirt set off with a bold matching trim that sits on the bottom edge. The shade is given extra fullness with the addition of an underskirt between the outer cover and the lining.

materials & equipment

frame with six struts and reverse gimbal fixture: 7 in. diameter top; 12 in. diameter bottom; 8 in. height

1 ³⁄₈ yd. lining fabric, 45 in. wide

1 ¹⁄₄ yd. toile de Jouy fabric, 55 in. wide

1 ¹⁄₂ yd. coordinating trimming, 1¹⁄₄ in. wide

¹⁄₂ in. wide binding tape

woven ribbons

Instead of using a panel of fabric, this novel shade is covered with a close basketweave of gingham ribbon. Here only one pattern of ribbon has been used, but you can choose any sort of ribbon or combination of colors to create your own individual woven shade. Adjust your measurements according to the width of the ribbons used and the size of the frame, and follow the simple weaving principle, finishing the top and bottom with a bright contrast trim.

materials & equipment

rectangular frame with long sides and reversible top gimbal: 10½ x 5 in. bottom; 6½ x 3 in. top; with 10 in. long sides and 4 in. measurement across the middle, top and bottom

15 yd. gingham ribbon, 1 in. wide

1½ yd. contrasting bias binding, ½ in. wide

½ in. wide binding tape

fabric adhesive

table lamps

The choice of lampshades in this category is over-whelming. Styles include slender candlesticks topped with tiny shades; half shades ideal for setting at each end of a mantelpiece or on a narrow shelf; heavy urnlike bases carrying sizable shades that may sit on a coffee or side table to provide pools of soft, atmospheric light; reading lights set upon a desk; or pretty bedside lamps suitable for the bedroom.

left A white plaster base with a cone shade laminated with a bright blue polka dot weave. *below from left* White dotted Swiss, finished with a ruffle; a generous Provençal cotton skirt, gathered with a bow; floral cotton, laminated onto a coolie shade and held on a classical glass column base.

above A tall turned base, topped with a gathered shade in thin blue cotton.
right This versatile brass table lamp is designed for maximum maneuverability and has a precisely pleated shade.

above Pretty and practical: a tilt-top desk lamp with a collared shade is finished with a gathered double ruffle.

left, top to bottom A gathered coolie with a difference—pale yellow silk is knife pleated and finished with blue binding, which is picked up by the matching wide two-tone fringe; striped fabric, neatly box-pleated over an Empire shade, is finished with complementary bias binding; a narrow tapered oblong is a good shape to use when there is not much space available, such as on a mantelpiece or on a windowsill.

above Polka-dot voile, tightly gathered over this Empire shade, lets out maximum light; the top and bottom edges of this shade have been stylishly finished with pinch-pleated silk and a contrasting color threaded through it.

below A traditional double chandelier lamp is updated with a pair of blue-and-white stripe gathered shades.

box-pleated conical shade

Hiding an ordinary conical shade is this perky box-pleated cover
made from a warm red and yellow *toile de Jouy*. The skirt falls in loose,
unstructured folds, allowing the pattern of the fabric to remain visible.
The bow is a pretty feature, highlighting the waist of the shade and
the ruffled effect of the gathered box pleats at the top.

materials & equipment

*frame with six struts and reverse gimbal fixture: 5 in. diameter top;
10 in. diameter bottom; 7 in. height*

20 in. lining fabric, 45 in. wide

1 ⅝ yd. toile de Jouy fabric, 45 in. wide

½ in. wide binding tape

t
p

11.

smocked patterned shade

A pretty blue Provençal skirt with a smocked top is slipped over a plain lined shade; the elasticized top means the cover stays firmly in place. Choose any motif pattern as an alternative. The great thing about this practical design is that it can be removed easily to shake off the dust or for washing.

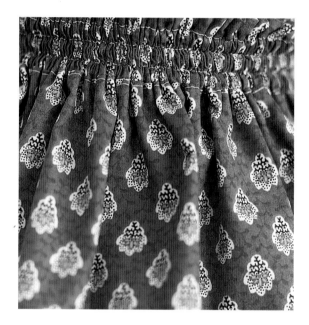

materials & equipment

frame with eight side struts: 6½ in. diameter top; 10 in. diameter bottom; 7 in. height, including 1½ in. collar

1 ³⁄₈ yd. lining fabric, 45 in. wide

20 in. Provençal cotton, 60 in. wide

½ in. wide binding tape

1 ⁵⁄₈ yd. elastic, ¼ in. wide

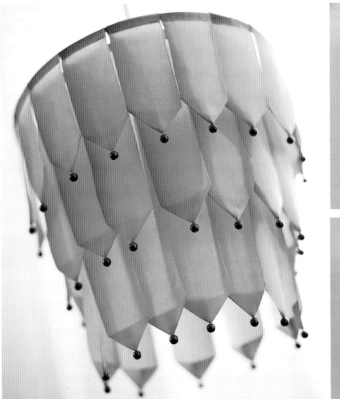

clockwise from top Layered taffeta ribbons finished with beads; wall sconces in velvet and pale checked cotton; a period brass wall bracket with a gathered cotton shade; yellow laminated burlap on a pendant drum shade; metal eyelets with rings attach a loose shade to a circular frame; pretty printed floaty voile is gathered tightly on a collared pendant.

Thin yellow cotton was dipped in fabric stiffener and then draped over a paneled shade. The molded shape was then finished with a satin tassel.

This fun harlequin chandelier was knitted from fine yellow silk yarn and draped over a ring frame. Gilt coins catch the light and keep the shade in shape.

A tightly knitted pagoda-shaped pendant, stretched over a series of ring frames, makes a most effective and clever overhead light fixture.

wall and ceiling lamps

Ceiling lights tend to operate as main sources of light, often illuminating a whole room. Although they should be capable of casting plenty of light, they should also be a decorative feature and draw the eye up. Wall lights come as uplights, bracket lights, and sconces, and are useful for throwing light onto surrounding surfaces to reflect back into the room.

above Thin gray and cream striped voile is tightly gathered to form a dense cover on a circular wall shield, which curves gently to hide the bulb from view on each side. A flame retardant lining is used to prevent scorching.
left A wall sconce throws light in a wide arc up to the ceiling and creates a wonderfully subtle effect. This one is laminated with rich yellow crushed velvet and edged with a laced leather thong.

linen
loose cover

An ornate wall sconce is topped with a piece of the palest
apricot linen no bigger than a pocket handkerchief. The soft-hued,
fluid fabric sits loosely on a cardboard shade and looks as if it has just
floated down and settled in place, creating a gentle pool of
background light for a relaxed and intimate atmosphere.

materials & equipment

*card undershade with bulb fitting: 3 in. diameter top; 7 in.
diameter bottom; 5 ¼ in. height*

20 in. apricot linen, 45 in. wide

pattern paper

compass, or pencil, drawing pin and string

gingham in gathers

For a lampshade like this miniature square, a small-scale pattern such as gingham is ideal. To give the tiny shade a little more impact, the fabric has been very tightly gathered all around the top and bottom, and matching braid has been attached to finish the edges and add a decorative touch.

materials & equipment

*square frame with four side struts and clip fixture: 3 ¹/₂ in. square top;
5 in. square bottom; 4 in. height*

20 in. blue and white gingham, 45 in. wide

20 in. white silk lampshade lining, 45 in. wide

¹/₂ in. wide binding tape

1 ¹/₄ yd. decorative braid

fabric adhesive

striped
wall shield

This minute half shade is designed to shield a bulb on a wall sconce.
The unusual shape is ideal for elaborate and ornate sconces. The
striped silk taffeta is stretched very tightly around the frame, and the
same stripe is cut on the bias to trim the edges. The whole project is
made with hand stitching only.

materials & equipment

half cylinder frame with bulb clip: 6 ¹/₂ in. wide; 5 in. height at center;
4 ¹/₂ in. height at sides

30 in. striped silk taffeta, 45 in. wide

10 in. lining fabric, 45 in. wide

curtains
and drapes

use of fabrics

Fabric comes in a wide and dazzling array of colors, textures, and patterns. By piecing together fabric in unexpected combinations, you will achieve innovative and original effects. Be adventurous, and experiment with contrasting textures and different designs, all cunningly combined in a single pair of draperies. Creative and imaginative use of fabrics will enable you to make elegant, stylish, and totally unique curtains.

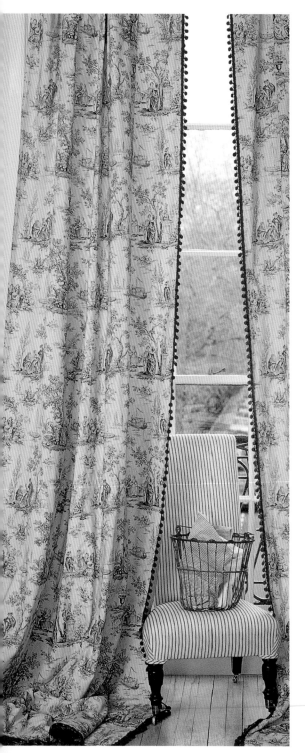

left Black and white antique *toile de Jouy* drapes are teamed with an irreverent red bobble fringing to create a timeless look at an elegant window. Unexpected combinations like this will enliven a simple pair of curtains. *above* Inexpensive slubby cotton has been lined and interlined for a luxurious and opulent effect. The bobble border at the top of the curtains creates textural interest.

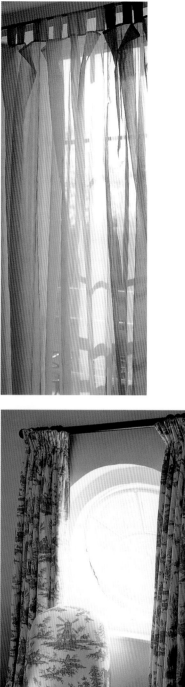

above A stylish alternative to the ubiquitous white sheers. A red and white voile check serves the same purpose—privacy—but with a little more verve and color.
above right Ready-made tab-topped curtains are dyed orange, yellow and red. The fabric filters light and creates a dappled effect.

above Crisp white cotton allows light to filter into a room, yet provides both privacy and shade.
right Two pairs of curtains on separate poles, one made from flimsy voile and the other cotton moiré, create an interesting layered look.

above The narrow edging on these pretty *toile de Jouy* curtains brings definition to the leading edge and frames an unusual round window. An upholstered slipper chair has been covered in the same fabric and continues the feminine yet unfussy theme.

yellow checks

These cheerful, colorful yellow curtains are guaranteed to bring
a relaxed, sunny atmosphere to any room, even in the darkest depths
of winter. They use three panels of coordinating fabric joined
horizontally. Vivid scarlet braid is sewn to conceal
any unsightly seams on the front of the curtain. The bold checks
and braid have a pleasing rustic simplicity that is echoed by the
simple ties that hold the curtains to an iron pole.

materials & equipment

three different main fabrics

lining fabric

⅝ in. wide red braid

contrast-bordered linen

These classic pencil pleat curtains have an unexpected feature—a deep border at the hem, in the same fabric but in a different color, which just rests upon the ground. Adding contrast borders is a simple yet effective device, for they bring color and variation to the plainest of curtains and add interest to a neutral, understated color scheme.

materials & equipment

main fabric

contrasting fabric for the border

lining fabric

3 ¼ in. wide pencil pleat header tape

curtain hooks

A variety of headings:
above left Red-checked voile
with a cased heading for
a softly gathered effect.
top Pinch pleats create an
elegant, formal feel.
above Gathering tape gives
a gently ruffled heading.
left A crisp check curtain
with neatly knotted ties.

headings

A curtain is attached to a track, rod, or pole by the heading—the decorative top of the curtain. From formal pleated headings hung from antique poles with elaborate gilt finials to informal ties loosely knotted around an iron rod, the heading sets the mood for the curtains. A wide variety of header tapes is now available, so creating pinch pleats, goblet pleats, soft gathers, and many other heading styles is now easier and more achievable than ever before.

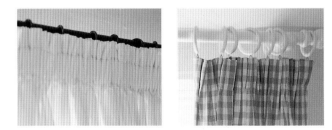

above left A tightly gathered pencil pleat heading gives
a ruched effect that adds interest to plain cream curtains.
above right A simple heading with rings attached to hooks.
right Unusual double curtains are attached to a pair of poles
by means of clip-on curtain rings, which require no sewing.

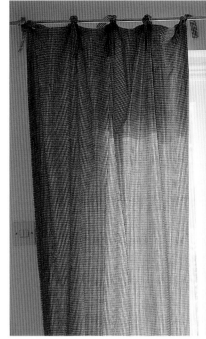

Top, above, and *right*
Three examples of knotted ties. This is a simple and informal style of heading that works very well when curtains are not too heavy. Curtains with a tie heading must be drawn by hand.
right Sunshine yellow ticking with a tiny loop heading is strung across the bottom half of a window on string tied to brass-headed nails.
below right Slotted onto a length of vivid red braided string, this checked curtain with a casing has a casual utilitarian feel.
below left A simple cream curtain hanging from a classic wooden pole is enlivened by the addition of a chenille bobble fringe all along the loosely gathered heading.

147

reversible scallops

These cozy quilted curtains could not be simpler to make.
The fabric is reversible, so the curtains do not need a lining, and
the scalloped top of the curtain simply flops over to act as a valance,
showing the other side of the fabric. The curtains are attached
to the pole with unobtrusive clip-on brass curtain rings, dispensing with
the need for a sewn heading. The contrasting binding adds
definition to the deeply scalloped edges of the valance.

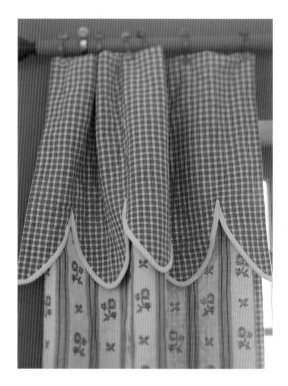

materials & equipment

reversible fabric

bias binding

clip-on brass curtain rings

tie-on sheers

These floaty unlined voile curtains hanging at a low casement window
create a light and airy atmosphere. The wrought-iron pole is
attached not to the window frame but to the ceiling, and the length
of the curtains and the swathes of fabric emphasize rather than
obscure the fine proportions of the elegant glass doors.
The tassel fringe provides a textural contrast with the economical
outlines of the simple metal holdback.

materials & equipment

white voile

tassel fringe

left This panel of fabric acts as a valance at a small kitchen window. Small-scale red-and-white gingham has a casing into which an expansion rod has been inserted. The fabric is held out of the way with thin ties, a quick and easy window treatment that need not be a permanent fixture.

below left A bold gothic-inspired valance covered in a rich red linen. This type uses buckram, a stiffened burlap fabric, which can hold the desired shape. Shaped and stiffened valances such as this one are guaranteed to add an air of importance to a window treatment and are especially useful for screening an unsightly window top.

below right A checked voile valance is edged top and bottom with thin red trim, which emphasizes the tight ruffles of the gathering-tape heading. Valances are ideally suited to windows that do not need a full curtain.

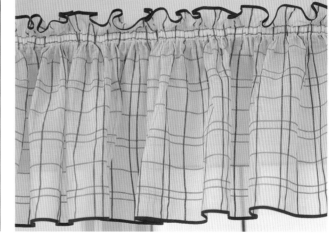

left A more traditional and formal valance treatment. A wooden board has been covered tightly with fabric that matches the curtains, then attached to the wall just above the curtain track on a pair of brackets. The box-pleated skirt has been either stapled or velcro'd to the board. The valance is trimmed with narrow binding in a color that complements the curtains.

valances

Valances add a perfect finishing touch to an attractive window treatment. Valances can either be stiffened, shaped pieces of fabric attached to a board, or softer in effect and gathered. They can be suspended from a pole, track, or rod and used alone or teamed with matching or contrasting curtains and drapes.

above This cheerful checked curtain is self-valanced—the valance is a separate piece of the same fabric sewn to the top of the curtain. Header tape has been attached to the back of the curtain just below the seam. A contrasting border defines the leading edge of the curtains and the bottom of the valance.

above right An unassuming pair of striped cotton curtains is made much more imposing by the addition of a classic shaped valance. Vertically striped curtains and valances can appear to lengthen the proportions small, wide windows.

right In a small bathroom, the window is screened by a sheer fabric panel and deep valance, which do not block the light as conventional curtains would. The bold valance is made from large-scale gingham check and edged with small-scale gingham cut on the bias.

157

monogrammed linen valance

This linen valance has been decorated with a machine-embroidered initial, but its fluid folds and majestic proportions would be just as effective if it were plain. The valance is designed to hang alone, but can be combined with unlined curtains in the same fabric suspended from eyelets screwed into the bottom of the valance board.

materials & equipment

heavy linen fabric

lining fabric

staple gun

¾ in. thick plywood for the valance board

angle brackets

rope-edged valance

The jolly stripes, wavy bottom, and coordinating rope trim
of this slightly gathered valance give it a cheerful nautical air. It is
an ideal summer replacement for heavy full-length curtains, which
are perfect for the winter months but can appear oppressive and
cumbersome during warmer weather. The valance allows plenty
of summer sunlight to flood into the room, yet prevents the
window from looking too bare and unfurnished.

materials & equipment

striped cotton fabric

thick rope trim

edgings

Adding an edging or border to a curtain will create an additional decorative element and subtly enliven even the most understated window treatment. From discreet scallops to tassel trimming, edgings should be chosen to complement yet contrast with your curtain. And always remember that bold and simple edgings are more effective than fuss and flounce.

below A translucent voile panel edged with wide grosgrain ribbon screens the view yet does not obscure the elegant lines of this window and full-length shutters.
top right The backs of curtains are rarely as attractive as the fronts. However, these are decorative on both sides. The front of the curtain is cheerful blue gingham while the back has a bold border. *center* and *bottom right* Shaggy silk fringe attached to the leading edge brings a an intriguing tactile quality to a plain pair of curtains.

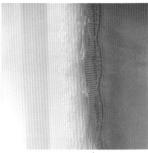

below, right, and *below right*
When used as an edging, bobble fringe adds an interesting textural element to any fabric furnishing and will instantly transform even the dullest pair of curtains. It is available in a wide variety of colors and weights, making it a suitable trimming for almost every fabric. Attached to the leading edge of a curtain, it will add definition and interest.

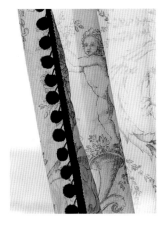

above These two striped panels screening the bottom half of a sash window are edged with a wide border cut from a contrasting check in the same color.
right A printed border sewn to the bottom of plain cotton curtains imitates the effect of handstitched embroidery.
far right A simple pair of floaty voile curtains are given an opulent, elegant feel with the addition of a fluffy tasseled fringe.

squares on squares

Bold borders add a simple yet extremely effective decorative
element to a pair of plain cotton curtains. Ideally suited to a small or
recessed window, the cheerful check borders make the curtains
into a focal point without swamping the window in folds of fabric.
Unobtrusive ties in the same checked fabric as the border hold the
curtains to a thin metal pole with heart-shaped finials that contribute
to the overall air of harmonious simplicity.

materials & equipment

heavy cotton fabric

cotton check for the border and ties

contrast-scalloped border

An elegant scalloped black felt border provides a striking textural contrast to the crisp clean folds and snowy white cotton of these floor-length curtains. The border adds definition to the pale curtains and frames the view from the window. The curtains are lined and interlined to give them a luxurious padded thickness.

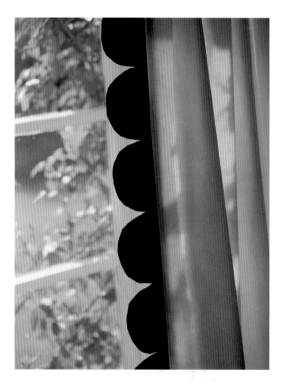

materials & equipment

white herringbone cotton

interlining

lining fabric

thick black felt

2 in. wide pencil pleat header tape

curtain hooks

equipment and techniques

BASIC EQUIPMENT

Sewing Kit
For the projects in this book you will need some basic sewing tools. A pair of good-quality fabric shears is essential, as are medium-sized dressmaker's scissors and small embroidery scissors for snipping threads. Pinking shears are useful for finishing raw edges. A metal tape measure, yardstick, and a small plastic ruler, will enable you to measure up accurately. Invest in good-quality steel dressmaking pins, which will not rust or blunt, and keep them in a box so they stay sharp. A variety of needles, for different weights of fabric, is also essential. Choose your needle according to the weight of the fabric and and the thickness of the thread, and keep a special needle just for embroidery. A steam iron is invaluable during the assembly process, but protect delicate fabrics with a damp cloth. Other useful items to have on hand are a quick-unpick to unpick seams, a blunt knitting needle for pushing out corners, and a thimble.

The projects in this book involve both hand and machine stitches. Basic proficiency in using a sewing machine is necessary, for although it is possible to make many items by hand, it would be a long and laborious process. Your sewing machine should have a good selection of basic stitches. Sophisticated accessories are not needed, but a zipper foot is required for some of the projects in this book. Finally, the process of making home furnishings will be much easier and more enjoyable if you work in a well-lit and well-ventilated area and have a large worktable.

Fabrics
In each project, the fabrics are specified, as the weight, texture, and pattern is suited to the particular design. If you want to use an alternative material, select fabric of a similar weight. Always try to choose fabric that is preshrunk and fade-resistant.

You can find cleaning instructions printed on the selvages of most fabrics in the form of care symbols. Any lined or interlined items must always be dry cleaned, as lining fabric and main fabric tend to shrink at different rates when washed.

The fire-retardant qualities of upholstery fabrics are governed by legislation in many countries. We suggest that you obtain advice from the manufacturer or the retailer of your chosen fabric to make sure your fabric is in line with these regulations.

bed linen

Measuring for bed linen
Before you embark on any of the projects in this book, you must first accurately measure the bed that the item is intended to furnish. This is essential as it will enable you to calculate the size of the finished item and figure out how much fabric you will need to make it. Always take measurements with a metal tape measure (plastic ones can stretch and become inaccurate) and enlist the help of an assistant if the bed is a large one.

Measuring for a pillowcase
Measure the width and length of the pillow. Add 10 ½ in. flap and seam allowance to the width and 1 ¼ in. to the length, unless otherwise stated in a project.

Measuring for a bedspread
Measure the bed with bedclothes and pillows in place. For the length, measure from the head to the floor at the foot of the bed.

Add an extra 12 in. to tuck behind the pillows. For the width, measure from the floor on one side of the bed over the bed to the floor on the other side. Seam allowances are given in the individual projects.

Measuring for a dust ruffle
Measure the bed base without the mattress. For the length of the central panel (which lies under the mattress), measure

the head to the foot of the bed. For the width, measure from one side of the bed base to the other. For the depth of the skirt, measure from the top of the bed base to the floor. The amount of fabric required for the skirt will depend on the desired fullness of the dust ruffle. Seam allowances are given in the individual projects.

Measuring for bedhangings and curtains
If you have a four-poster bed, measure the drop from the bottom of the horizontal supports to the floor for the length of the

bedhangings, and the distance between the vertical supports for the width. If you wish to make a corona or other wall-mounted bed draperies, it is much easier to measure and calculate fabric quantities once the pole or corona board is in place. As a rough guide, they should be positioned approximately 12 in. below the ceiling, but this measurement may have to be adjusted, depending on the proportions of the room. Attach any hardware securely to the wall, using sturdy brackets that will be able to bear the weight of the fixture plus several yards of fabric.

Cutting out the fabric

When making bed linen, or indeed any home furnishings, the fabric must be cut straight, or the finished item will hang crookedly. Unfold the fabric on a flat surface. Use a drafting square and metal ruler to mark a straight line in pencil or fabric pen across the width on the wrong side of the fabric. To cut a width of fabric in half, fold it selvage to selvage and press, then cut along the pressed fold line. If you are using fabric with a high sheen or pile, mark the top of each width with a notch so you can make sure all the fabric will run in the right direction on the finished item.

Joining widths

When making duvets, sheets, or bedspreads, always place a full width panel in the center of the item with equal part or whole widths joined on each side. To join widths, place the widths together, right sides facing, and machine stitch using a $\frac{5}{8}$ in. seam. Trim the surplus fabric.

TEMPLATES FOR BED PROJECTS

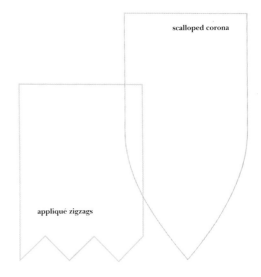

scalloped corona

appliqué zigzags

cushions and pillows

Pads and fillings

Ready-made pillow forms come in a variety of different shapes and sizes. There are also several different fillings. The most luxurious filling is a combination of feather and down, which should be used sparingly in a puffy scatter cushion or more densely to stuff a firm seat cover. Plastic or latex foam chips tend to be lumpy and uncomfortable, but they are non-absorbent and so are useful for outdoor furnishings. Foam blocks can be cut to size and are used to form squabs for seating; cover the blocks with batting first to smooth out the corners. If you make your own pillow form with a feather filling, use a downproof fabric such as a thick, close-weave cotton, or the sharp feather ends will protrude. Plain cotton or muslin fabric is suitable for pads with a synthetic filling. Do not allow feather or synthetic pads to get wet because they are very absorbent.

Fabrics for cushions and pillows

Choose the type of fabric according to the function of the cushion. Use general upholstery fabrics for most throw pillows, tougher cloth for floor, outdoor, upholstery or squab cushions, and delicate fabrics for more decorative pillows. Try to use preshrunk, colorfast fabric, so you can wash your cover if needed. If you want to use an unusual fabric, check how much it is likely to shrink when washed, since you may need to buy up to a third more material to allow for this process.

TEMPLATES FOR CUSHION PROJECTS

autumnal appliqué

lampshades

Frames

There are all manner of shaped frames to choose from. Traditionally, frames were made of wire and then painted or covered with bias binding to prevent rusting, but today most are plastic-coated. When selecting a frame, make sure the style and size are appropriate to the proposed base. You can re-cover an old frame with new fabric if you strip away the old cover, but make sure there are no defects in the basic outline. Shown below are a selection of the most popular frames available with their technical names. You can also buy rings of different diameters, which can be combined with fabrics stiffened by lamination to make cone-shaped frames. This method allows for greater flexibility in shape and size than with ready-made wire cone frames.

Measuring and marking tools

Accurate measuring and marking are essential aspects of lampshade making, as it is vital to make sure the cover fits neatly on the frame. Use a metal rule for straight edges and a tape measure for curves and longer lengths. For measuring and drawing small circles, use a compass. For larger circles, make your own compass using a piece of string or tape. Insert a thumbtack pin through one end to mark the midpoint of the circle and attach a pencil to the other end. Adjust the length of string or tape according to the diameter you require and pivot the pencil around the pin to draw the circumference. Thick paper or cardboard is ideal for making templates. For more difficult shapes it is easier to make the template by pinning a lining material or thin muslin directly onto the frame to make sure of a close and accurate fit. Use an ordinary pencil, dressmaker's chalk, or a removable fabric marker for marking the pattern.

Adhesives

Work with an appropriate adhesive; use fabric adhesive for joining fabric to fabric and multipurpose glue for attaching all other types of surfaces, such as laminated fabric to a frame. Clothespins are handy for holding glued edges together while drying.

Laminated covers

Stiff covers are made by laminating a fabric with a self-adhesive backing. Slowly peel away the protective paper from the backing and on a flat surface carefully press the wrong side of the fabric to the sticky surface, removing any trapped air by smoothing with your hands from the middle out. Stiffen the fabric first and then cut out the required pattern. Self-adhesive backing is not suitable for use on an openweave fabric because dust gathers between the threads.

Fabric covers

The type of material you choose will affect the quality of light shed by the shade. White and light solid colors radiate maximum light, while dark colors and patterns obscure light. Stick to smaller repeats since large-scale patterns will be lost on all but the biggest shades. Lightweight cotton and silk are ideal for tight-fitting shades as they have give in them to aid stretching onto the frame. Geometric patterns such as checks should be cut and applied on the bias since it is difficult to achieve really straight vertical and horizontal lines. By positioning the checks at an angle, the eye will not detect a slight lack of symmetry. Try to use an economical width of fabric for the shade, or piece panels together, pattern matching as necessary. Fabric on a shaped frame will fit better if it is first cut into smaller pieces and then joined into panels. Pleated and gathered covers are deceptive; they require a lot more fabric than tight covers, often two or three times as much, so calculate amounts carefully and allow for seam allowances when you are joining pieces together.

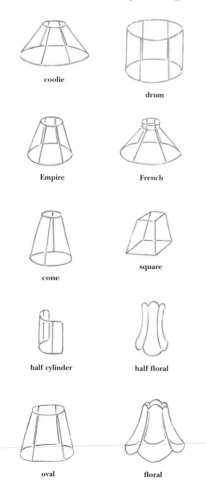

coolie

drum

Empire

French

cone

square

half cylinder

half floral

oval

floral

Linings

These are generally used in white or cream to allow for maximum reflection of light. The lining helps to hide the struts and the outline of the bulb. Use a strong, non-tear, heat-resistant fabric such as fine Shantung or Japanese silk, satin or crepe. Acetate is a good alternative, although this is more liable to tear. Flame-retardant spray is available for treating the lining. No lining is required on a laminated shade or when you use very heavy fabrics, but with lightweight fabrics like voile or lace, lining is essential to help diffuse light and give substance to the cover.

Trimmings

Many lampshades are finished with a trimming, to hide unsightly stitching, finish raw edges, and provide decoration. Bobble fringe, braid, ribbon, rope, tassels, and piping are just some options, and they can be glued or handsewn in place. Measure the section to be trimmed with a tape measure and add at least 1 in. to finish the ends. For removable covers, check the washability and dyes of the trimming. It is a good idea to prewash all fabrics and trimmings before making the cover, to insure even shrinkage and to avoid colors running into each other.

Fixtures

When you have decided on the size and shape of your frame, you must consider the internal fixtures that hold the frame on the support; these are available in various sizes. Your choice of fixture will depend on the function of the shade: for instance, a pendant fixture is necessary for hanging shades, whereas a reversible gimbal is used on table lamps, allowing them to be tilted when directing light on specific areas. Converters and shade carriers are available if you wish to change the height or use of your shade. Finally the size of your bulb can affect the fixture—the bulb must be hidden from view and sit at a safe distance from the lining to avoid scorching or a fire hazard.

Bulbs

Choose a bulb according to the fixture and the size and style of the shade. The bulb should sit below the level of the top of the shade and not hang below the bottom of the shade. The bulb should be at least $1\frac{1}{4}$ in. away from the inside of the shade. Be very careful that the bulb does not come closer than this distance, or scorching may occur. The bulb must also be set properly in the fixture to avoid burning. For larger lampshades, use up to 60-watt bulbs, but on smaller shades choose 40-watt or below. Low-voltage bulbs are long lasting and give a bright light and low heat.

TECHNIQUES

Binding the frame

Binding the frame not only gives a better finish if the shade is seen from above or below, but it also provides a necessary anchor for attaching the fabric cover. In most cases, it is best to use a white or neutral-colored binding, although sometimes a different color may suit the design.

First make sure the frame is the correct shape and free from bends, as any defects will show. Use $\frac{1}{2}$ in. wide binding tape. To calculate how much tape is needed, first measure the length of all the sections to be covered with a tape measure and double the final measurement. To bind the frame, spiral the tape all the way around the frame, always maintaining the same angle and just overlapping each previous wrap. Do not overlap by too much or the binding will become very thick and bulky. The finished binding should have a tight, smooth finish so that when you twist it between thumb and index finger it does not slip or move.

To bind a strut, cut a length of binding tape twice the length of the strut. Turn 1 in. of the tape over the top ring and with the cut end pointing down, spiral the tape down. Finish at the base of the strut with a knot.

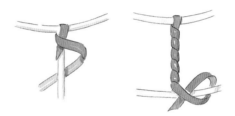

To bind the top and bottom rings of the frame, start by binding a cut end under itself immediately next to a side strut. When you reach a joint with a strut, neatly work the tape around it in a figure-eight pattern. To finish the loose end, fasten with tiny hand stitches and trim away the excess binding.

Measuring the frame

To measure any kind of cone-shaped frame, or one that has angled sides, you must first calculate the circumference of the openings at the top and the bottom of the frame by measuring the relevant diameter (the width across each opening) and then multiplying this figure by three. The height of the frame is the angled (not the vertical) height between the top and bottom rings.

curtains and drapes

Measuring the window

Before starting to make curtains, you must first measure the window to calculate how much fabric is needed. This is a very important calculation, so take your time and check your measurements

again once you have finished.

If possible, mount the track, pole, or valance board in place before measuring the window. The track or pole should be attached 2–6 in. above the window frame, with the ends projecting at least 4 in. beyond each side of the window. Take measurements with a metal tape measure, and if the window is very tall or wide, get someone to help you.

The two measurements needed to calculate fabric quantities for a pair of curtains are the width and the length of the window. To calculate the width of the finished curtains, measure the width of the track, rod, or pole. If you are using a valance board, measure the sides and front. To calculate the drop of finished full-length curtains, measure from the top of the track or bottom of the pole to the floor. For sill-length curtains, measure from the top of the track or bottom of the pole to the sill. For apron-length curtains, measure from the top of the track or pole to just below the sill or to the desired point.

Calculating fabric quantities

Length

The drop from the track, pole, or rod to the floor, sill, or other desired point will determine the length of the finished curtains. Add the appropriate heading and hem allowances (given in the individual projects).

Width

The amount of fabric required is dictated by the curtain heading. Pencil pleat header tape, for example, requires fabric that is two and a half times as wide as the track or pole. Add the allowances for hems and joining widths (given in the individual projects).

To calculate how much fabric you will need for a pair of curtains:

1. Multiply the length of the track or pole by the heading requirement (2 ½ for pencil pleat heading) to reach the final fabric width.
   E.g. Length of the track or pole = 6 ft.
   Pencil pleat heading = 2.5 x length
   Width of fabric = 200 x 2.5 = 5 yd.

2. Divide this measurement by the width of your fabric to calculate how many widths of fabric are required. Round up the final figure to the next full width.
   E.g. Width of chosen fabric = 54 in.
   Width of fabric needed = 196 in.
   196 divided by 54 = 3.6
   Rounds up to 4

3. Multiply this figure by the unfinished length of the curtain to find out how much fabric is needed.
   E.g. Working drop = 10 ft.
   10 x 4 = 40
   Therefore, the total length of fabric required is 40 ft., 20 ft. for each curtain.

Allowing for pattern repeats

To match a pattern across a pair of curtains, you need to know the length of the pattern repeat (the fabric supplier will be able to provide you with this information). Divide the unfinished length of each curtain by the length of the repeat, round up the result to the next full figure, then multiply it by the length of the repeat to find out how much fabric you will need.
E.g. The unfinished length of your curtain (including allowances) is 60 in.
The pattern repeat is 25 in.
60 divided by 25 = 2.4
Rounded up to 2 ½
2 ½ multiplied by 25 = 62 ½
Each cut length must be 62 ½ in. long.

Heading requirements

A few standard heading requirements:

Gathering tape

2–2.5 times length of track

Pencil pleat tape

2.5–3 times length of track

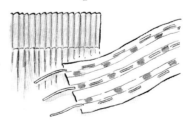

Ties

1–2 times length of track

Cased heading

2–3 times length of track

Cutting out the fabric

It is essential that the fabric is cut straight, or the curtain will hang crooked. Place the fabric on a flat surface. Use a metal ruler and a drawing square to mark a straight line in pencil or fabric pen on the wrong side of the fabric. Cut along the line. To cut a width in half, fold it selvage to selvage and cut along the fold. If you are using fabric with a high sheen or pile, mark the top of each width with a notch so all the fabric will run in the right direction on the finished curtain.

Joining widths

Always place any half widths at the outside edge of the curtain, with a full width at the leading edge. To join two widths, place them right sides together, and pin, baste, and machine stitch a straight seam ⅝ in. from the raw edges. Trim away any surplus material. If the fabric puckers, it is best to unpick the seam and start again.

Matching patterns across joined widths

On one width of the patterned fabric, fold under a ⅝ in. seam allowance to the wrong side and press. Lay the other piece of fabric on a flat surface, right side up. Place the fabric with the folded edge on the second piece of fabric and carefully match the pattern. Pin in place across the fold.

Calculating the size of a valance board

A valance board should be approximately 5–7 in. deep, so the curtains project far enough beyond the window. It must be the width of the window frame plus 4 in. to give clearance at each end.

Making a valance board

Using a small saw or jigsaw, cut a piece of plywood or composite board to the required proportions and sand any rough edges. Attach a pair of angle brackets to the underside of the board. This is now the back edge. Two brackets will support a short board; use three or four brackets if you have a long or heavy board.

If the board is visible behind the curtains, it must be covered. Cut a piece of matching fabric large enough to cover the board, lay it on a flat surface, wrong side up, and place the board in the center. Fold the fabric over the board as if it were a present and staple it neatly in place, using a heavy-duty staple gun. Use a drill to attach the board firmly to the wall.

TEMPLATES FOR CURTAIN PROJECTS

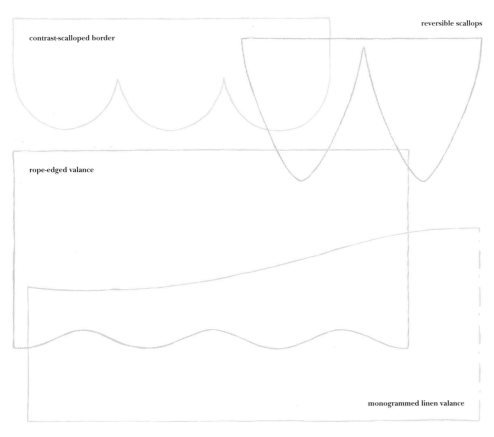

contrast-scalloped border

reversible scallops

rope-edged valance

monogrammed linen valance

basic sewing techniques

STITCHES

Basting stitch

This temporary stitch is like a larger, looser version of running stitch. It holds fabric in place until it is permanently stitched. Use a contrasting thread so the basting is clearly visible and easy to remove.

Running or gathering stitch

A series of small, neat stitches, equal in length on both sides of the fabric. Running stitch is used to gather cloth by hand. Knot the thread at one end and sew two parallel rows of running stitches close together along the length to be gathered. Wind the loose threads at the other end around a pin and pull gently to form even gathers.

Slipstitch

Slipstitch holds a folded edge to flat fabric or two folded edges together, as in a mitered corner. Work on the wrong side of the fabric, from right to left. Start with the needle in the fold. Push it out and pick up a few threads from the flat fabric, then insert it into the hem again, all in one smooth and continuous movement. When finished, the stitches should be almost invisible.

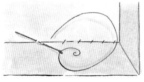

Herringbone stitch

This stitch is used to hold a raw edge to flat fabric. Work from left to right on the wrong side of the fabric, with the needle pointing from right to left. Start with the needle in the hem. Push it through the hem and bring the needle diagonally up to the flat fabric. Take a small backward stitch in the flat fabric, about ¼ in. above the hem, picking up just a couple of threads. Bring the needle diagonally back down to the hem, then make a small backward stitch through one thickness of the fabric. Keep the stitches loose.

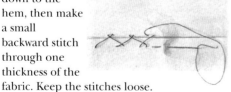

Hem stitch

Hem stitch should be used to join fabric to the binding tape wrapped around a lampshade frame or to hold a folded edge to

a flat fabric. Catch a couple of threads from the flat fabric, then with the needle pointing diagonally from right to left, slide it under the fabric and bring it up through the binding tape.

Buttonhole stitch

This stitch is used for buttonholes or wherever a raw edge needs to be finished or strengthened. Work on the right side of the fabric and stitch with the raw edge of the buttonhole uppermost. Push the needle through the fabric, from back to front, approximately ⅛ in. below the raw edge. Twist the thread around the tip of the needle then pull the needle through to form a knot at the raw edge of the fabric. Always keep the stitches evenly spaced.

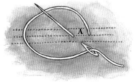

Cross stitch

Where possible, work decorative cross stitches in a row, first stitching one half of the cross, then returning back along the row to complete the stitch.

Feather stitch

This decorative stitch should be worked on the right side of the fabric. Bring the needle through at A, insert at B, and bring through again at C, looping the thread underneath the needle before pulling it through. Mirror the process by inserting the needle at D, coming out again at E, and looping the thread underneath the needle again. Repeat this pattern, alternating the looped stitches on each side of the central line.

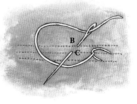

SEAMS

Flat seam

This seam is used to join pieces of fabric. Place the two pieces of fabric right sides together, aligning the edges that are to be seamed. Pin and baste, then machine stitch the seam. Reverse the stitches at the beginning and end of the seam to secure it in place.

Flat-fell seam

This is a sturdy seam for joining heavy fabric. Pin the fabrics right sides together and baste along the seam line. Machine stitch the seam, then press it to one side. Trim the underneath seam to half its width. Fold the upper seam allowance over the trimmed one and baste. Machine stitch in place close to the folded edge.

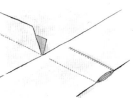

French seam

This self-finishing seam contains all raw edges and is used for sheers and lightweight fabrics. Place two pieces of fabric wrong sides together, aligning the raw edges that are to be seamed. Pin, baste, and machine stitch a seam close to the raw edge. Trim the seam. Fold the material right sides together and then pin, baste and machine stitch a second seam ½ in. from the first, enclosing the raw edges in a narrow tube of fabric.

Double hem

A double hem encloses raw edges and lies flat against the back of fabric. For a 4 in. double hem, the hem allowance will be 8 in. Press the hem allowance along the edge of the fabric. Open out the hem and fold the raw edge up to the pressed line. Fold up again and stitch in place.

Mitering corners

Mitering is the neatest way of working hem corners. Press the hem allowance along the bottom and sides of the fabric then open it out flat again. Where the two fold lines meet, turn in the corner of the fabric diagonally. Turn in the hems along the pressed fold to form a neat diagonal line. Use slipstitch to secure.

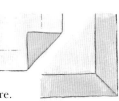

Making an angled miter

An angled miter is necessary when a double bottom hem is wider than the side hems. Press the hem allowance along the bottom and sides of the fabric, then open out again. Fold the corner of the fabric in toward the bottom hem. Then make the first fold in the double hem. Fold in the side hem, then make the second fold in the double hem. The folded edges should meet.

Making ties and tabs

To make a tie, cut a strip of material to the desired width and length. Fold the strip in half along the length, wrong sides together, and press. Pin, baste, and machine stitch all along the long side and one short end, leaving the other short end unstitched. Push the tie right side out with a knitting needle. Turn in a ¼ in. fold to the inside of the tie, press in place, and slipstitch the end closed. Tabs are made in exactly the same way—the only difference is that strip of fabric is wider and they are often buttoned, not tied.

Cutting fabric on the bias

Place your chosen fabric on a flat surface, wrong side up. Take one corner and fold it so the end of the fabric is aligned with the selvage, forming a triangle of fabric. The diagonal fold line is the bias line of the fabric.

Making bias binding

Bias binding is an effective and attractive way to enclose raw edges of fabric. It is easy to make. Find the bias line of the fabric as described above, then mark lines parallel to the bias line across the fabric. Cut out the strips and join them to make a continuous strip of bias binding.

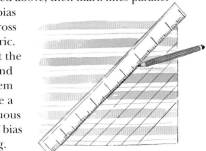

Place two
strips, with
their right
sides together,
at right angles,
lining up the raw edges.

Then machine stitch the two strips together, using a ¼ in. seam allowance. Press flat and cut off the corners.

Making cording

Cording is made from a length of piping cord covered with bias binding. The bias binding must be wide enough to cover the cord and to allow a ⅝ in. seam allowance on each side of it. Wrap the binding around the cord, right side out, then machine stitch close to the cord, using a zipper foot.

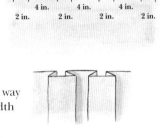

Making box pleats

Box pleats give a tailored finish to curtains, valances, and cushions. One box pleat requires fabric three times the width of the pleat. Decide on the finished width of each pleat, then multiply it by three. The finished width of the object you are making must be divisible by this measurement. For example, if each pleat is 4 in. wide, the width of the item to be pleated must be exactly divisible by 12 in. If it is not, you will have to adjust either the width of the object or the width of the pleat.

For a 4 in. pleat, mark a fold 2 in. from the edge of the fabric and another 2 in. from that. Then mark alternate 4 in. and 2 in. folds across the top of the fabric. Fold along the first mark, 2 in. from the edge of the curtain, and bring it across to join a mark 8 in. away from it. Pin the folds together. Leave a 4 in. space and repeat the action all the way across the width of the fabric.

credits

Endpaper: bed linen from Harrods
Page 1: *top left:* lampshades made by Acres Farm, fabric from Ian Mankin; *top right:* voile from John Lewis, fixtures from Antiques & Things; *below left:* fabric from F. R. Street, piping from V. V. Rouleaux; *below right: from left to right* cushion from Liberty, cushion made by Hikaru Noguchi, cushion made from fabric by Colefax and Fowler
Page 2: fabric from Designers Guild
Page 4: *above left:* interior design by Reed Creative Services, all fabrics through Reed Creative Services; *above right:* fabric from Sanderson, tension wire kit from IKEA
Page 5: *above left: from l–r:* shade made by Robert Wyatt, fabric from JAB, base from Mr Light; shade and base from Purves & Purves, shade made by Vaughan, fabric from Knickerbean, base from Bella Figura; shade made by Bella Figura, fabric from Parkertext, base from Vaughan; shade and base from Mr Light; *above right:* check fabric by Schumacher from Turnell & Gigon
Page 6: *above left:* blue-and-white floral shade made by Robert Wyatt, fabric from Design Archives; *below right:* ready-made curtains from Inventory
Page 7: *above left:* quilt from Nicole Fabre; *below right:* all cushions from Cath Kidston

BED LINEN

Pages 8–9: fabric from F. R. Street, velvet piping from V. V. Rouleaux

Pillows and sheets, pages 10–19
Piqué pillows with bows: both fabrics from McCulloch & Wallis
Red-trimmed linen: fabric from Designers Guild, trimming from V. V. Rouleaux

Bedspreads, pages 20–29
Appliquéd quilted bedspread: fabric from Sanderson, striped cotton from F. R. Street
Feather stitched patchwork quilt: made by Tobias and the Angel

Valances, pages 30–39
Tailored pictorial print: fabric from Christopher Moore Textiles
Appliquéd zigzags: plain fabric from Malabar Cotton Company, checked fabric from Designers Guild

Canopies, pages 40–49
Scalloped corona: checked fabric from Ian Mankin, valance fabric from Osborne & Little, corona from The Blue Door
Tie-on bed curtains: fabric from Shaker

CUSHIONS

Pages 50–51: *left to right:* cushion from Liberty, cushion made by Hikaru Noguchi, cushion made from fabric by Colefax and Fowler

Shapes, pages 52–61
The Star: fabric from Chelsea Textiles
Bobbles in the round: fabric from The Conran Shop, bobble fringe from Jane Churchill

Use of fabrics, pages 62–71
Stripes into squares: fabric by Schumacher from Turnell & Gigon, tassel from Wendy Cushing
Ribbon weave: made by Hikaru Noguchi

Trimmings and fastenings, pages 72–85
Rope-edged knotted cushion: inspired by Wendy Harrop, fabric from Ian Mankin, rope border from John Lewis
Fastened with tassels: inner fabric from Manuel Canovas, outer fabric from John Lewis, tassels from Wendy Cushing
Loose linen cover: fabrics from Sanderson, ties from John Lewis

Surface decoration, pages 86–91
Autumnal appliqué: fabrics from John Lewis

LAMPSHADES

Pages 92–93: shades made by Acres Farm, fabric from Ian Mankin

Shapes, pages 94–99
Pleated coolie: made by Sally Harclerode, silk from Pongees

Use of fabric and trimmings, pages 100–109
Skirted pictorial print: made by Bella Figura, fabric from Baer & Ingram, trimming from Jane Churchill
Woven ribbons: made by Robert Wyatt, ribbon from V. V. Rouleaux

Table lamps, pages 110–119
Box-pleated conical shade: fabric from Manuel Canovas, base and shade by Vaughan
Smocked patterned shade: shade from The Dining Room Shop

Wall and ceiling lamps, pages 120–133
Loose linen cover: made by Hänsi Schneider, fabric from Sahco Hesslein
Gingham in gathers: shade by Vaughan, fabric from Ian Mankin, trimming from V. V. Rouleaux
Striped wall shield: shade by Sally Harclerode, fabric from Manuel Canovas

CURTAINS

Pages 134–135: voile from John Lewis, fixtures from Antiques & Things

Use of fabrics, pages 136–145
Yellow checks: fabrics from Ian Mankin, trimmings from V. V. Rouleaux
Contrast-bordered linen: antique linen from Nicole Fabre, curtains by Reed Creative Services

Headings, pages 146–155
Reversible scallops: fabric from Pierre Frey
Tie-on sheers: fabric from JAB, pole made to order

Valances, pages 156–165
Monogrammed linen valance: fabric from F. R. Street
Rope-edged valance: fabric from Designers Guild, rope trim from V. V. Rouleaux

Edgings, pages 166–175
Squares on squares: plain fabric from Sanderson, checked fabric from KA International
Contrast-scalloped border: fabric from F. R. Street, felt from Muraspec, pole from Artisan

Page 184: *top left:* fabric from Sanderson, trimmings from John Lewis; *top right:* lampshade from The Blue Door; *below left:* both fabrics from KA International; *below right:* antique bolster from Pimpernel & Partners

Page 192: bedhangings from John Lewis, bed and sheets from Shaker

directory of suppliers

PILLOWS

ABC Carpet & Home
888 Broadway
New York, NY 10003
212-473-3000

Bloomingdales
1000 Third Avenue
New York, NY 10022
212-705-2000

Charlotte Moss
1027 Lexington Avenue
New York, NY 10011
212-772-6244

Nicholas
979 Third Avenue, Suite 1015
New York, NY 10021
212-688-3312

Pillow Finery
979 Third Avenue
New York, NY 10022
212-752-9603

The Pillowry
P.O. Box 6902
New York, NY 10128
212-308-1630
By appointment only

Pottery Barn
Stores nationwide.
Call 800-838-0944 or visit
www.potterybarn.com for details of your
nearest store.
Free catalog available.

HOME FURNISHINGS

ABC Carpet & Home
see under Pillows for details

Ad Hoc Softwares
136 Wooster Street
New York, NY 10012
212-982-7703

Bed, Bath and Beyond
Stores nationwide.
Call 800-GO-BEYOND or visit
www.bedbathandbeyond.com
for details of your nearest store.
Free catalog available.

Calico Corners
203 Gale Lane
Kennett Square, PA 19348
800-213-6366
Free catalog available

Calvin Klein Home
Available from selected stores nationwide.
Call 800-294-7978 for details of your nearest
retailer.

Donghia Home Furnishings
979 Third Avenue
New York, NY 10022
212-935-3713

Gracious Home
1992 Broadway
New York, NY 10023
212-231-7800
www.gracioushome.com

Ralph Lauren Home Collection
980 Madison Avenue
New York, NY 10021
212-642-8700

Pottery Barn
see under Pillows for details

John Rosselli International
523 East 73rd Street
New York, NY 10021
212-772-2137

John Rosselli International
523 East 73rd Street
New York, NY 10021
212-772-2137
212-772-2137

LAMPSHADES

Laura Ashley
Call 212-496-5110 or visit
www.lauraashley.com for details.

Just Shades
21 Spring Street
New York, NY 10012
212-966-2757

Mainely Shades
100 Gray Road
Falmouth, ME 04105
207-797-7568

Oriental Lampshade Company
816 Lexington Avenue
New York, NY 10021
212-832-8190

Ruth Vitow
155 East 56th Street
New York, NY 10022
212-355-6616

Vaughan
979 Third Avenue
New York, NY 10022
212-319-7070
To the trade only.

FABRICS and TRIMMINGS

B & J Fabrics
263 West 40th Street
New York, NY 10018
212-354-8150

Pierre Deux French Country
870 Madison Avenue
New York, NY 10021
212-570-9343

Lou Lou Buttons
69 West 38th Street
New York, NY 10018
212-398-5498

M & J Trimmings
1008 Sixth Avenue
New York, NY 10018
212-391-9072

Rosen & Chadick Fabrics
246 West 40th Street
New York, NY 10018
212-869-0142
www.rosenandchadick.com

Silk Trading Co.
360 South La Brea Avenue
Los Angeles, CA 90036
800-854-0396
www.silktrading.com

Thai Silks
252 State Street
Los Altos, CA 94022
Call 800-722-7455 for details of your nearest
retailer.

Tinsel Trading Co.
47 West 38th Street
New York, NY 10018
212-730-1030

CURTAINS

Country Curtains
At The Red Lion Inn
Dept. 54100
Stockbridge, MA 01262
800-937-1237

Crate and Barrel
Stores nationwide.
Call 800-967-6696 or visit
www.crateandbarrel.com for details.

Kirsch
P.O. Box 0370
Sturgis, MI 49091
Call 800-528-1407 for details.

Shannon & Jeal
722 Steiner Street
San Francisco, CA 94117
415-563-2727

BED LINENS

Aria Fine Linens
214 Park Avenue South
Winter Park, FL 32789
407-628-2021

Bella Linea Nashville
6031 Highway 100
Westgate Shopping Center
Nashville, TN 37205
615-352-4041

Fortunoff
The Mall at the Source
1300 Old Country Road
Westbury, NY 11590
516-832-9000
www.fortunoff.com

Lassiter's Bed N' Boudoir
3500 Peachtree Road
Atlanta, GA 30326
404-261-0765

Linens Limited Inc.
113 Clay Avenue
Lexington, KY 40502
Call (888) 3-Linens or visit
www.linenslimited.com
for details of your nearest store.

glossary

Appliqué Applying a second layer of fabric to a main fabric, usually with decorative stitching.

Batting Thick, soft padding material, made from natural or synthetic fibers, and used for upholstery and quilting.

Bias binding A strip of cloth cut on the bias, at 45° to the selvage, which gives stretch to the fabric. Used as an edging, to bind frames, or to cover piping cord.

Bobble fringe Tufted ball attached to a length of trimming.

Bolster A long cylindrical pillow or cushion with flat ends.

Box pleat A flat, symmetrical pleat formed by folding the fabric to the back at each side of the pleat.

Braid A woven ribbon used for trimming or edging an item.

Buckram Coarse cloth, stiffened with size and used to give rigidity to valances.

Casing A curtain heading in which a sleeve of material is left open at the top of the curtain to receive a curtain rod or pole.

Chenille Tufted and soft velvety yarn; wool, cotton or synthetic.

Corona A circular or semicircular structure mounted on the wall above a bed or sofa with draperies suspended from it.

Cotton A natural fiber made from the boll of the cotton plant.

Dust ruffle A skirt of fabric that runs around the base of a bed to hide the legs.

Felt Unwoven cloth made from pounded wool; the edges do not fray after cutting.

Finial A decorative fixture attached to each end of a curtain pole.

Flange A flat rim or border running around a pillow or cushion.

Gathers Puckers or folds made by pulling gently on a loosely stitched thread.

Gaufrage A pattern branded onto the surface of velvet.

Gimbal The device attached to the inside of a lampshade frame that holds the shade on the base or the bulb.

Gingham A plain-weave two-color cotton cloth with a check pattern.

Heading The top of a curtain, finished with tape, ties, rings, or other treatments.

Header tape Ready-made tape that is attached to the top of a curtain to create a particular heading.

Interlining Soft material, used as backing or inner lining, gives a luxurious quality.

Knife pleat A narrow, sharply folded pleat with a straight edge.

Laminate A thin protective covering, bonded to a material.

Linen A strong and flexible fabric spun from the fibers of the flax plant.

Lining fabric A secondary fabric used to back curtains, valances, and bedspreads to protect them from light and dust. Usually a cotton or synthetic sateen fabric with a slight sheen.

Madras cotton Striped and checked fine Indian cotton, usually in bright colors.

Matelasse A thick double cotton cloth, stitched at regular intervals to create a luxurious quilted effect.

Miter The neat diagonal joining of two pieces of fabric where they meet at a corner.

Organdy A fine, sheer, fabric made with cotton yarns.

Organza A stiff, transparent fabric.

Pencil pleat heading A popular curtain header tape that creates regular, stiff pleats.

Piping A length of cord covered with bias binding and used as a decorative edging.

Piqué A type of weave that produces a hard-wearing cloth with a ribbed texture and crisp finish.

Pleat A fold or crease that has been pressed or stitched in place.

Provençal print French country print on cotton, characterized by small motifs.

Raw edge The cut edge of fabric, without selvage or hem.

Ruffle A gathered strip of cloth used as a trimming.

Seam allowance The narrow strip of raw-edged fabric that is left on each side of a stitched seam.

Seam line The line formed when two pieces of material are stitched together.

Silk A luxurious and soft yet strong fabric produced from a fiber spun by silkworms.

Strut A bar in a lampshade frame designed to brace and strengthen it against pressure.

Template A shape cut from cardboard or paper and used to mark specific outlines on fabric.

Ticking A striped, closely woven heavy cotton twill fabric, usually with a thin stripe.

Toile de Jouy Cotton cloth printed with pastoral scenes in a single color on a neutral background.

Topstitching A straight seam seen on the right side of the fabric.

Valance A strip of fabric or a fabric-covered board that runs across the top of a window.

Velcro A double tape used for closing fabrics. One piece of tape is covered with a synthetic fuzz while the other is covered with tiny nylon fiber hooks. When pressed together, the two fabrics cling together until they are torn apart.

Velvet A plush, luxurious warp-pile fabric with a short, closely woven pile. Can be made from cotton or synthetic fibers.

Voile A light, plain-weave cotton or man-made fabric. Suitable for sheer curtains and bed drapes.

Waist The narrow, middle part of a lampshade, often used to accentuate a flaring or pleated skirt.

Weave An interlacing action used to form something, such as a fabric.

Width The distance from selvage to selvage on any fabric.

index

acknowledgments

Producing a home furnishing book of this magnitude requires not only a huge amount of fabric, trimmings, and other sewing paraphernalia, but also very special skills that produce the best finishes. I have had invaluable help from many fabric companies who very generously donated many yards of fabric for the projects in this book. I have also benefited from the generosity of suppliers of lamps and shades, curtain poles and fixtures, beds and bed linens, and pillow forms and covers. Thank you, one and all.

James Merrell's beautiful photographs are the making of a book like this, and I owe him a big thank you for his ever-professional input and unflagging energy. To make the pictures as inspiring and accessible as possible, we photographed the furnishings in real homes, and I am very grateful to the people who so kindly allowed us to disrupt their lives and hang curtains, throw cushions, and scatter lamps and bedspreads around their houses. They include Isobel Bird, Liz Shirley, Anna Thomas, Susie Tinsley, Cath Kidston, Annie Stevens, Tim Leese, Bobby Chance, and Fiona Wheeler—many thanks to you all.

Hänsi Schneider, Helena Lynch, Celia Dewes, and Robert Wyatt have all been instrumental in the hand-crafting of many of the objects in this book—their work is exquisite and greatly appreciated.

Thank you to all at Ryland Peters & Small for another professionally produced book. The beautifully drawn illustrations that accompany the instructions are the work of Lizzie Sanders, Michael Hill, and Jaqueline Pestell, each of whom has produced work of the highest standard—many thanks.

Janey Joicey-Cecil and Catherine Coombes have both enabled me to work freely due to their continued support, help, and friendship. You are both truly appreciated.

Dedication

For my goddaughter, Kate Joicey-Cecil, in celebration of your 21st year and wishing you a happy and fulfilled adulthood.